Who Would Like a Christmas Tree?

By Ellen Bryan Obed

Illustrated by Anne Hunter

HOUGHTON MIFFLIN BOOKS FOR CHILDREN
HOUGHTON MIFFLIN HARCOURT
BOSTON NEW YORK 2009

For my husband,
who brought me into the land
of Christmas trees
—E.B.O.

For my son, Jamie,
who plays under the Christmas trees
all year round
—A.H.

Who would like a Christmas tree in January?

"We would like a Christmas tree in January," answer the black-capped chickadees.

"Our breakfast, lunch, and supper are in the Christmas tree. We hang upside down to look for moth eggs and little spiders hidden under the bark. We like to peck what's left over from the cones that were growing high in the tree. We find winged seeds in the crispy brown scales. What a feast!

"At night we roost together in the thick branches. We are tired from eating all day, so we fluff up our feathers and go to sleep."

Who would like a Christmas tree in February?

"We would like a Christmas tree in February," answer the field mice.

"We scurry along our secret winter runways in the plantation. We never hibernate. When we come to the trunk of a Christmas tree, we stop to nibble and gnaw. The bark is delicious! Besides, this is a comfortable place to eat, for no one can see us here—not the fox or the owl or the Christmas tree farmer. We are safe under a roof of snow."

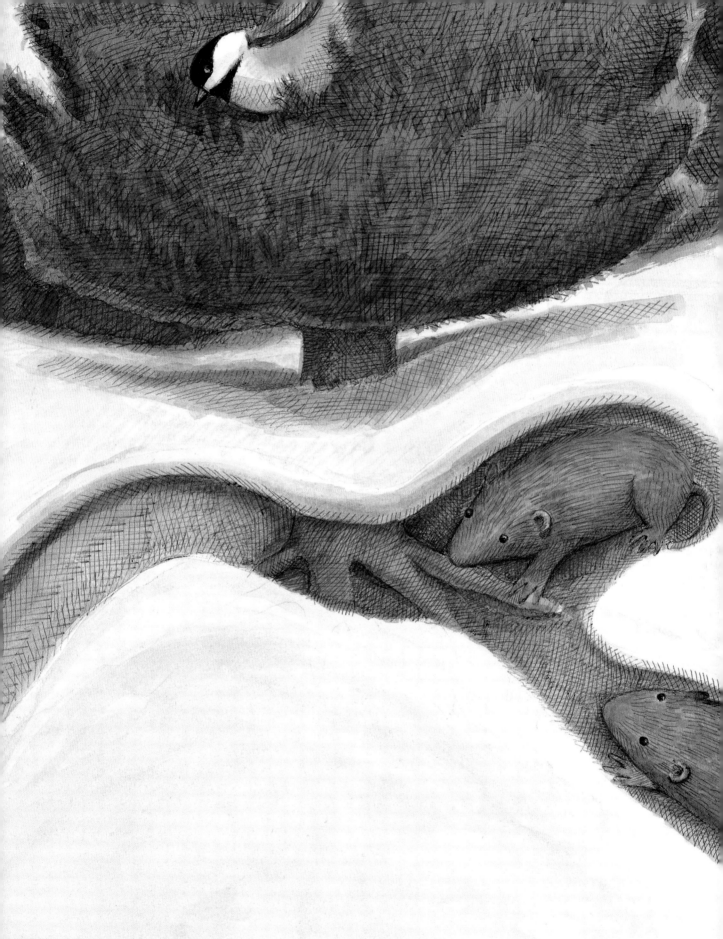

Who would like a Christmas tree in March?

"We would like a Christmas tree in March," answer the white-tailed deer.

"We are tired of being deep in the woods. We come out to the edge of the plantation to have a look around. We walk the rows and eat up and down the sides of the big trees. The first-year branches are very tender. The snow is beginning to melt, so we eat the tops of the young trees, too.

"We snack early in the morning and late in the day. We are bucks, does, and fawns feeding together in small groups. We take our time. Why hurry? It's easy trails and easy eating in the Christmas tree plantation."

Who would like a Christmas tree in April?

"**We would like a Christmas tree in April,**" answer the woodcock.

"The plantation is our Singing Grounds. We call just before dawn and again just after sunset from our low places in the grass.

"*Pzeent . . . pzeent!*

"We are the male woodcock. We perform Song Flights to attract our mates, spiraling up in the evening air one hundred meters into the sky. As we start to descend, we make excited chirps. Then we zigzag silently downward, diving and falling to a safe and quiet landing near the Christmas trees."

Who would like a Christmas tree in May?

"I would like a Christmas tree in May," answers the robin.

"I like to perch on the top of the Christmas tree and sing when the sun is coming up and when the sun is going down. From here I also look for food: caterpillars, worms, beetles, flies, and spiders. I hop everywhere on the ground near the trees, pulling up earthworms and grabbing bugs. I fly off with my bill full of food for my babies. They are waiting in the nest hidden in the hedgerow next to the plantation."

Who would like a Christmas tree in June?

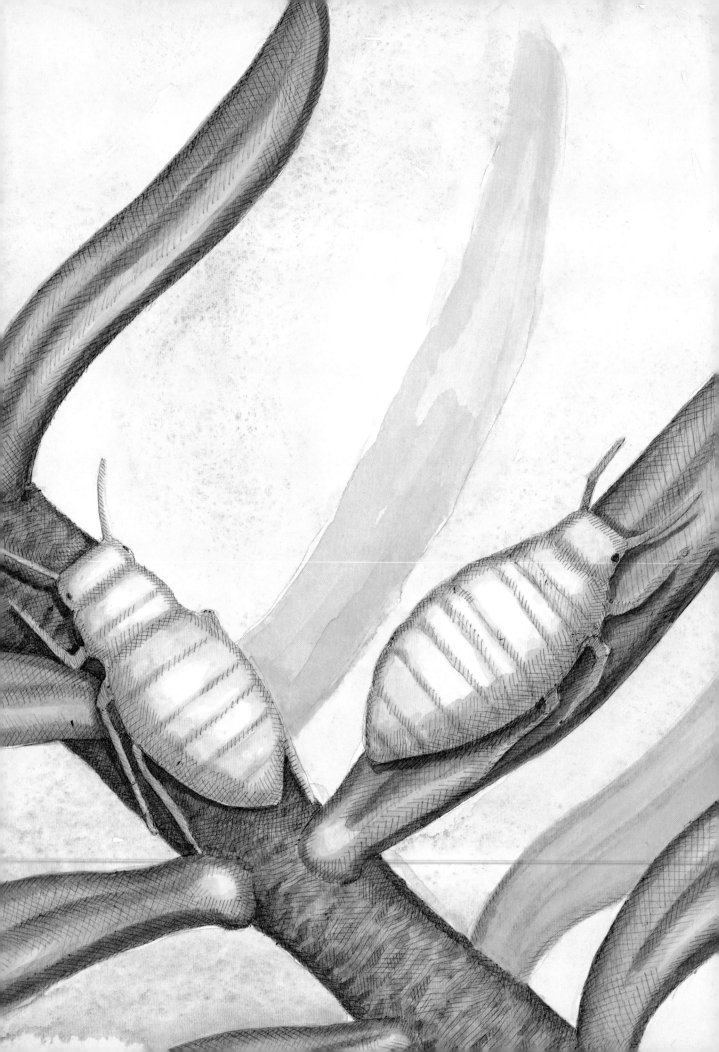

"We would like a Christmas tree in June," answer the balsam twig aphids.

"We come out of our tiny eggs that have been attached to the balsam fir twigs all winter and spring. We are pale yellow nymphs no bigger than the point of a pencil. We feed on the underside of old needles.

"Soon there are more of us . . . we move inside the bud . . . and more of us . . . we feed on new needles . . . and more of us! Now we are a colony of winged and wingless aphids. We are covered with white waxy wool and sticky honeydew that smells like brown sugar."

Who would like a Christmas tree in July?

"We would like a Christmas tree in July," answer the wildflowers.

"The soil where Christmas trees grow is the soil where *we* like to grow. Lots and lots of us crowd together between the rows and under the trees. Daisies and dandelions. Smartweed and bindweed. Shepherd's purse and Queen Anne's lace, evening primrose, wild radish, and grasses. Many kinds of grasses. We are everywhere and decorate the plantation with sweet blossoms and color."

Who would like a Christmas tree in August?

"We would like a Christmas tree in August," answer the monarch butterflies.

"We have spent our summer in the milkweeds that grow among the Christmas trees. We came out of our eggs from under the long, thick leaves.

"As caterpillars, we fed on the leaves, buds, and milky juice. We hung from the plants in green, golden-spotted chrysalises. Now we are out, and we are beautiful! All of us are getting ready to migrate south. But first, we feed on flowers and rest like delicate black and orange ornaments on the milkweeds and Christmas trees."

Who would like a Christmas tree in September?

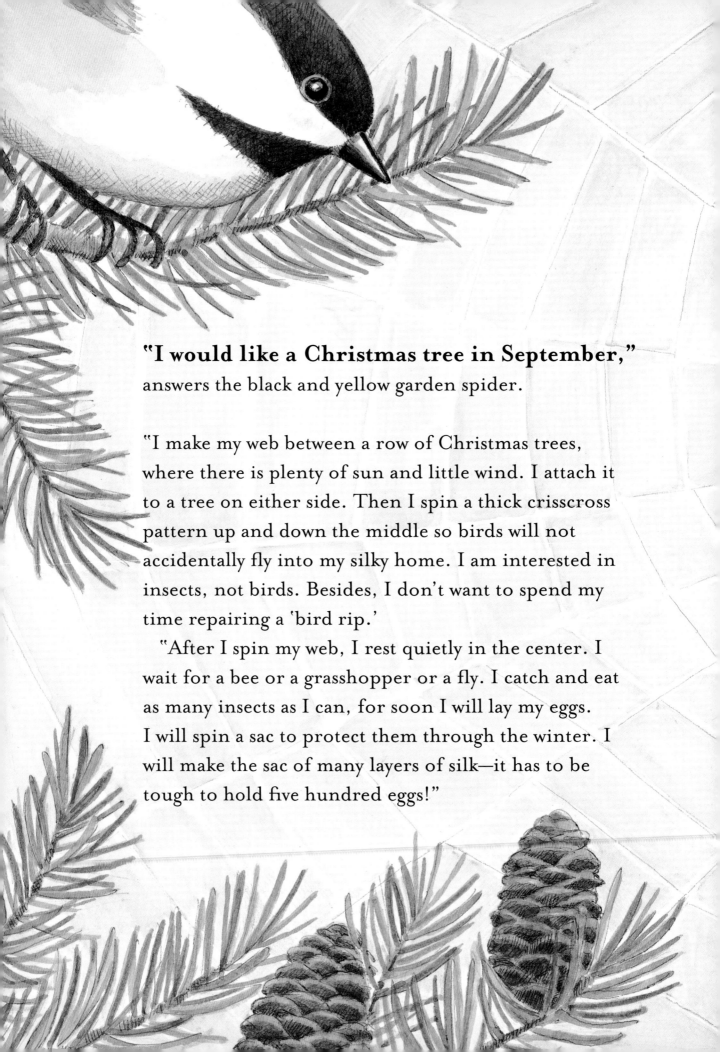

"I would like a Christmas tree in September," answers the black and yellow garden spider.

"I make my web between a row of Christmas trees, where there is plenty of sun and little wind. I attach it to a tree on either side. Then I spin a thick crisscross pattern up and down the middle so birds will not accidentally fly into my silky home. I am interested in insects, not birds. Besides, I don't want to spend my time repairing a 'bird rip.'

"After I spin my web, I rest quietly in the center. I wait for a bee or a grasshopper or a fly. I catch and eat as many insects as I can, for soon I will lay my eggs. I will spin a sac to protect them through the winter. I will make the sac of many layers of silk—it has to be tough to hold five hundred eggs!"

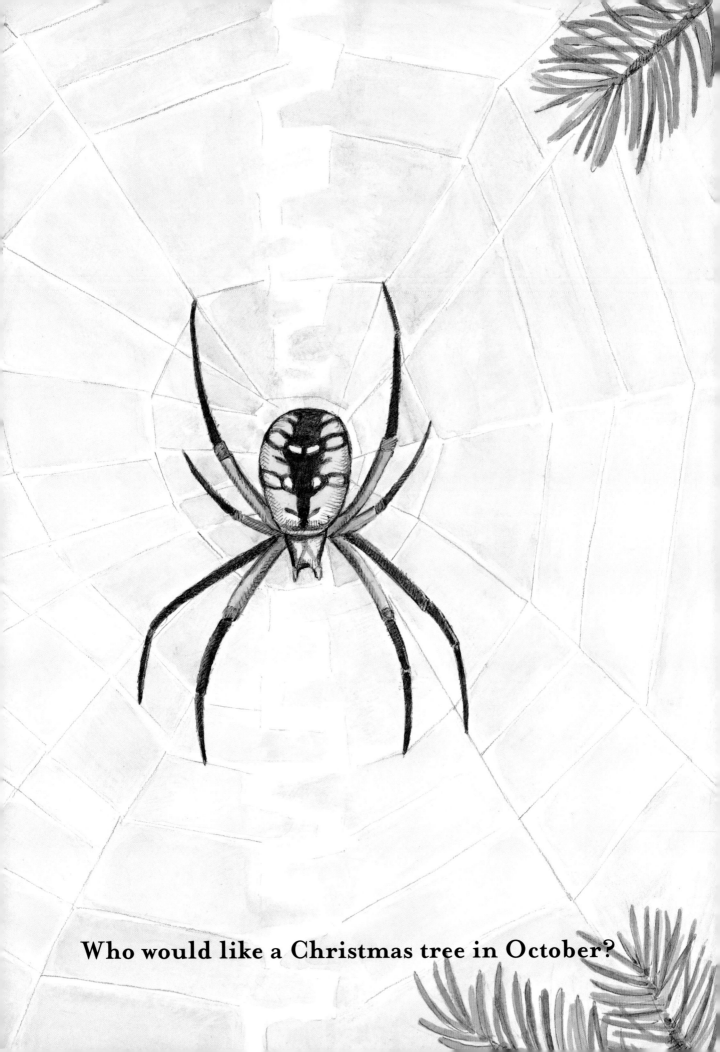

Who would like a Christmas tree in October?

"I would like a Christmas tree in October," answers the red fox.

"I could eat lots of things that live in the Christmas tree plantation in the fall—grasshoppers, crickets, little sparrows, a late crop of clover. But I come for mice. I can tell you that the plantation is full of mice. I know because I come here often. I hear them. I smell them. I see them.

   "I hunt by myself. I walk through the rows of trees without a sound. Tip-toe, pounce. Tip-toe, pounce. Tip-toe, *pounce!*"

Who would like a Christmas tree in November?

"We would like a Christmas tree in November," answer the wild turkeys.

"We are toms, hens, and poults clucking and purring as we search for food in the plantation. There are eighteen of us in our flock. We scratch for seeds, peck at roots, and eat grasses. We take dust baths to rid our feathers of mites.

"We also look for mound ants when the days are warm. We find them between the rows of trees. We scratch open the hills and eat the ants. Then we amble off to the nearby woods to fill up on acorns."

Who would like a Christmas tree in December?

"We would like a Christmas tree in December!"
answer the children and their parents.

"We go into the plantation to pick out our tree. We pull
it on a sled back to the warming shed. There we pay the
farmer, sip hot cider, and share spicy Christmas cookies.
The farmer helps us tie the tree to the roof of our car.

"'We hope you enjoy your Christmas tree,' she says as we wave goodbye.

"'We will!' we answer all together."

How the Christmas Tree Farmer Takes Care of Her Farm Around the Year

Trees grown on this Christmas tree farm are Balsam Firs (*Abies balsamea*) and Fraser Firs (*Abies fraseri*).

January

Black-capped Chickadee (*Poecile atricapilla*)
"My family and I ski up and down the rows in the snow-covered plantation. We like to watch the little chickadees. They help to keep the plantation healthy by eating some of the harmful insects that overwinter in the trees."

February

Meadow Vole or field mouse (*Microtus pennsylvanicus*)
"When we find mouse tracks on top of the snow, we know that the field mice are busy underneath, nibbling the trunks of the Christmas trees. When the snow melts, we will see what they have done! We hope they have not eaten all the way around the tree. The thin, soft layer between the inner bark and wood is called the cambium, or 'growing layer.' If they have eaten the cambium layer, the tree will die."

March

White-tailed Deer (*Odocoileus virginianus*)
"The deer come out of the woods in early spring. We shake a mixture of cloves, garlic, and dried meat meal up and down the rows of trees. The smell of these ingredients helps to keep the deer out of the plantation. We don't want them to help themselves to the tender branches of the Christmas trees."

April

American Woodcock (*Scolopax minor*)
"When we hear the woodcock's *'pzeent . . . pzeent,'* we know that spring is coming to the farm. We get ready to take care of our trees—planting, giving nutrients, mowing, cutting, and spraying early-hatching insects and weeds."

May

American Robin (*Turdus migratorius*)
"The robin perches on the top of one of the tallest Christmas trees in the plantation. So do crows, bobolinks, sparrows, goldfinch, and cedar waxwings. We stake out tall poles with perches so the birds will sit on them and not break the fragile tops of the trees."

June

Balsam Twig Aphid (*Mindarus abietinus*)
"Time to count aphids. I take my magnifying glass into the plantation. How many aphids will I find on one branch of a Christmas tree? 'One, two, three, four, five . . .' If there are more than twelve, we will have to spray the branches with a mist to prevent damage. No one wants to buy a Christmas tree with curled and twisted needles!

"We prune the lower branches of the trees. We cut them eight to ten inches from the ground. We want good air circulation around the base of the trees so ferns and fungi do not grow and mice will not build nests. And now the trees will have bare lower trunks or 'handles,' which will fit nicely into Christmas tree stands!"

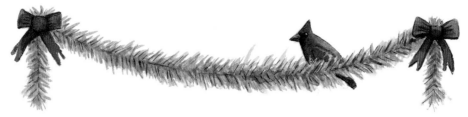

July

Ox-eye daisy (*Chrysanthemum leucanthemum*), Common Dandelion (*Taraxacum officinale*), Smart-weed (*Polygonum pensylvanicum*), Bindweed (*Convolvulus arvensis*), Shepherd's Purse (*Capsella bursa-pastoris*), Queen Anne's lace (*Daucus carota*), Evening Primrose (*Oenothera biennis*), Wild Radish (*Raphanus raphanistrum*), Barnyard Grass (*Echinochloa crusgalli*), Yellow Foxtail or Pigeon Grass (*Setaria glauca*), Witchgrass or "Tumble-weed" (*Panicum capillare*)

"We mow the wildflowers so they won't take the nutrients in the soil away from the growing trees. But first I pick some to put in the end of the tall, stiff black hose I put in front of my mower. The workers in other parts of the plantation see my flowers sticking up and know where I am.

"I also pick wildflowers to take home. Ox-eye daisies, purple clover, and Queen Anne's lace look pretty together in a vase on the kitchen table."

August

Monarch (*Danaus plexippus*), Common Milkweed (*Asclepias syriaca*)

"We shape the trees with shearing machines. We cut the tops off with hand clippers until there is one left; we call this top the leader. After the monarch butterflies come out of their chrysalises, we mow the milkweeds."

September

Black and Yellow Garden Spider (*Argiope aurantia*)

"We continue to shape the trees and cut out the extra tops. We work very close to the spiders in their webs. We don't want to hurt them, because they are catching insects that are harmful to the trees. But when I go down the rows of trees in my mower, I *do* disturb them. I put a bouquet of goldenrod and aster in the hose in front of my mower to catch the webs. I don't want to get covered with spider silk!"

October

Red Fox (*Vulpes vulpes*), Meadow Vole or field mouse (*Microtus pennsylvanicus*)

"We get ready to sell our Christmas trees. We measure them and tag them. Our dog, Blue, is with us. She is looking for mice. She hears them. She smells them. She sees them. Just like the fox, she loves mice! Sometimes she stands up on her hind legs to try to get a mouse that has scurried high into a tree for safety."

November

Wild Turkey (*Meleagris gallopavo*), Allegheny Mound Ant (*Formica exsectoides*)

"We hire extra workers who help us cut and tie the tagged trees. Big trailer trucks arrive to take the trees to faraway markets. One trailer truck can hold as many as 650 Christmas trees!

"We see turkeys in the plantation. They are scratching ant mounds and eating the ants. We are glad to see the big flock of hungry turkeys, because mound ants are a problem on the plantation. These ants like to make their mounds on ground that has no shade. When a tree is nearby, the ants sting it with formic acid. The formic acid damages the cambium or growing layer of the trunk, which causes the tree to die."

December

"The Christmas tree chosen by the family is a Balsam Fir (*Abies balsamea*). The greens used for making wreaths and garlands in the warming shed are Balsam Fir, Northern White Cedar 'eastern aborvitae' (*Thuja occidentalis*), and Eastern White Pine (*Pinus strobes*).

"Our welcoming shed is warm and fragrant. Workers make wreaths and garlands with fir and other evergreen branches. When customers arrive, we invite them into the shed for hot cider and Christmas cookies. We give them a map of the plantation, a handsaw, a measure, and a sled or cart.

"'We hope you find the perfect tree,' we say as they head off into the plantation."

Acknowledgments

To Cynthia Hall of Hall's Christmas Tree Farm in Sangerville, Maine,
who provided much information, many ideas, and the setting for this book.
Also to Clay Kirby, entomologist, University of Maine Extension Services,
for his help with species information and for reading over the manuscript.

Text copyright © 2009 by Ellen Bryan Obed
Illustrations copyright © 2009 by Anne Hunter

Houghton Mifflin Books for Children is an imprint of the Houghton Mifflin Harcourt Publishing Company.

www.hmhbooks.com

The text of this book is set in MrsEaves.
The illustrations are done in watercolor and ink.

Library of Congress Cataloging-in-Publication Data
Obed, Ellen Bryan, 1944–
Who would like a Christmas tree? / written by Ellen Bryan Obed ; illustrated by Anne Hunter.
p. cm.
Summary: Describes the flora and fauna that inhabit a Christmas tree farm throughout the year, using the growing trees
for a variety of purposes. Includes section on how the farmer takes care of the farm through the year.
ISBN 978-0-547-04625-9
[1. Christmas tree growing—Fiction. 2. Christmas trees—Fiction. 3. Trees—Fiction. 4. Nature—Fiction.] I. Hunter, Anne, ill. II. Title.
PZ7.O118Wh 2009
[E]—dc22
200805230

Manufactured in China
LEO 10 9 8 7 6 5 4 3 2 1